LET'S-READ-AND-FIND-OUT SCIENCE®

STAGE 1

From Tadpole to

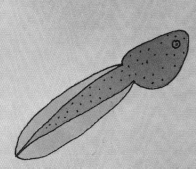

FROG

by
Wendy Pfeffer

illustrated by
Holly Keller

HarperCollinsPublishers

For Diane and Steve,
with love—
Children, like tadpoles, grow up so fast.—W. P.

With thanks to Dr. Edmund Stiles, Professor of Biological Sciences at Rutgers University, and Valerie Chase of the National Aquarium in Baltimore, for so kindly reviewing the manuscript; John Cooney of Rutgers for his much-needed assistance; the Wednesday Workshoppers for their valued comments; Renée Cho for her helpful guidance; and with special thanks to Tom for his patience.

The *Let's-Read-and-Find-Out Science* book series was originated by Dr. Franklyn M. Branley, Astronomer Emeritus and former Chairman of the American Museum–Hayden Planetarium, and was formerly co-edited by him and Dr. Roma Gans, Professor Emeritus of Childhood Education, Teachers College, Columbia University. Text and illustrations for each book in the series are checked for accuracy by an expert in the relevant field. For a complete catalog of Let's-Read-and-Find-Out Science books, write to HarperCollins Children's Books, 10 East 53rd Street, New York, NY 10022.

FROM TADPOLE TO FROG
Text copyright © 1994 by Wendy Pfeffer
Illustrations copyright © 1994 by Holly Keller

Library of Congress Cataloging-in-Publication Data
Pfeffer, Wendy, date
  From tadpole to frog / by Wendy Pfeffer ; illustrated by Holly Keller
    p.   cm. — (Let's-read-and-find-out science. Stage 1)
  Summary: Describes the metamorphosis from tadpole to frog.
  ISBN 0-06-023044-4. — ISBN 0-06-023117-3 (lib. bdg.) — ISBN 0-06-445123-2 (pbk.)
    1. Frogs—Development—Juvenile literature.   2. Tadpoles—Juvenile literature.   3. Amphibians—Metamorphosis—Juvenile literature. [1. Frogs.   2. Tadpoles.   3. Animals—Infancy.] I. Keller, Holly, ill.   II. Title.   III. Series.
QL668.E2P525 1994
597.8'9—dc20

93-3135
CIP
AC

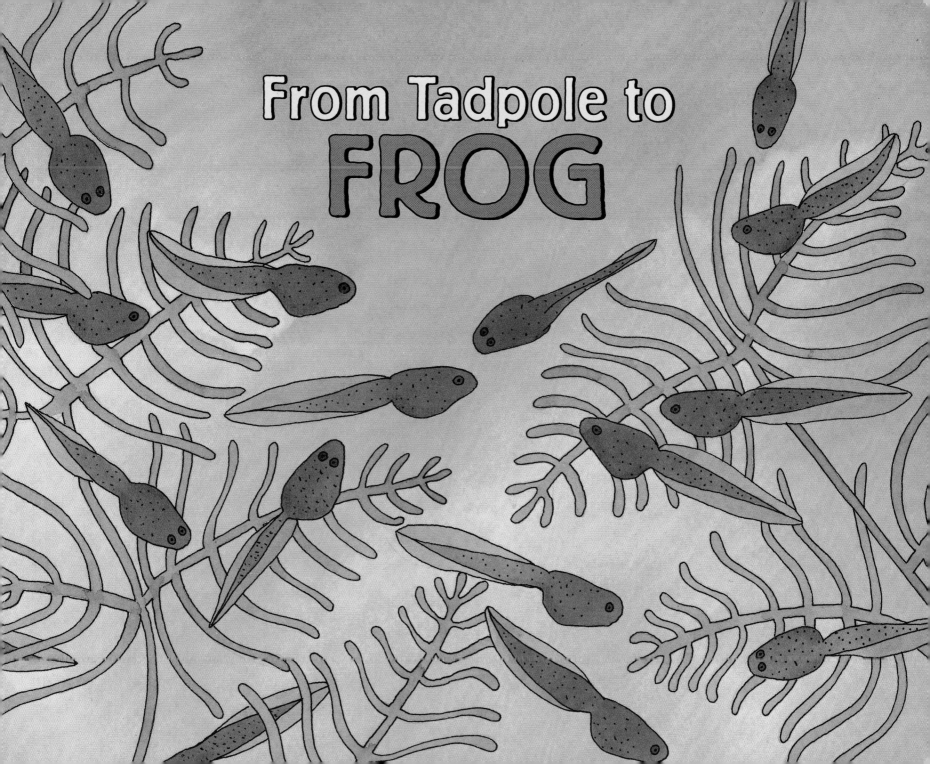

From Tadpole to
FROG

4

This is Frog Pond.
But where are the frogs?

When winter winds whistle, the frogs hide. They sleep at the bottom of the pond in the soft mud. Frogs hibernate in their hideaway all winter long.

After the ice melts, flowers appear. Birds return. And pond creatures wake up.

Spring has arrived at Frog Pond. Here are the old frogs stretching their legs.

At night you hear "Ba-ra-rooom . . . ba-ra-rooom . . . ba-ra-rooom . . ." The males are calling to their mates.

The females hear the call.

The male hugs his mate. He fertilizes her eggs as she lays them in the water. Thousands of soft jelly-covered eggs cling together in the cool water.

In about ten days the eggs hatch. The pond comes alive with thousands of tiny tadpoles. They wiggle their tails and breathe underwater with gills, just like fish.

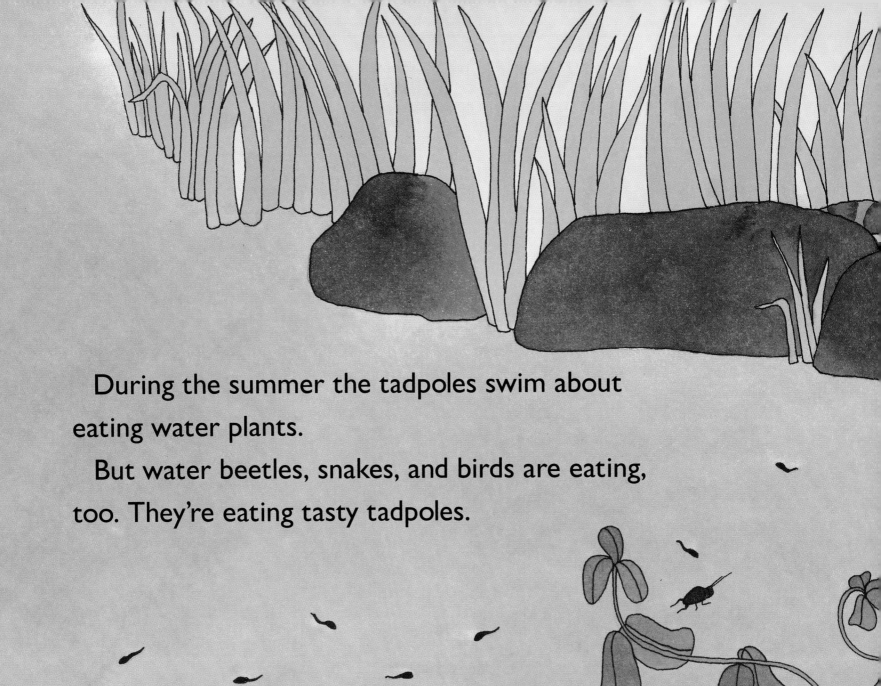

During the summer the tadpoles swim about
eating water plants.

But water beetles, snakes, and birds are eating,
too. They're eating tasty tadpoles.

When fall comes, look carefully in the water. Are any tadpoles left?

Look here! Are they tadpoles or wet leaves? They're brownish-speckled tadpoles. Hundreds of them float by with the brownish-speckled leaves. Eating and swimming, swimming and eating, the tadpoles grow fat.

When winter winds blow again, they burrow
under the mud at the bottom of the pond.
They do not eat.
They do not move.
They just sleep.

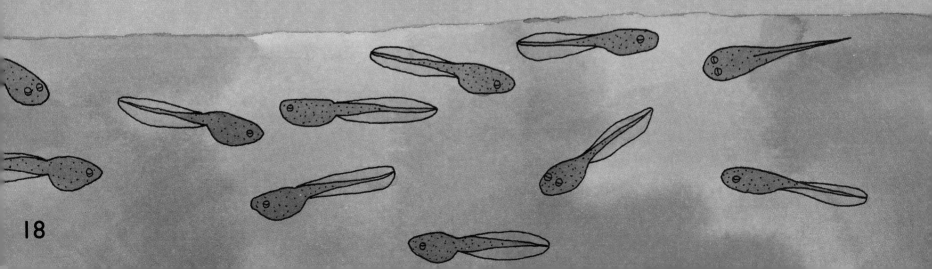

When spring sunshine warms the tadpoles' world, they awake . . . hungry.

So they swim and eat, eat and swim.

Tiny hind legs begin to sprout. They grow longer and stronger while the tail grows shorter.

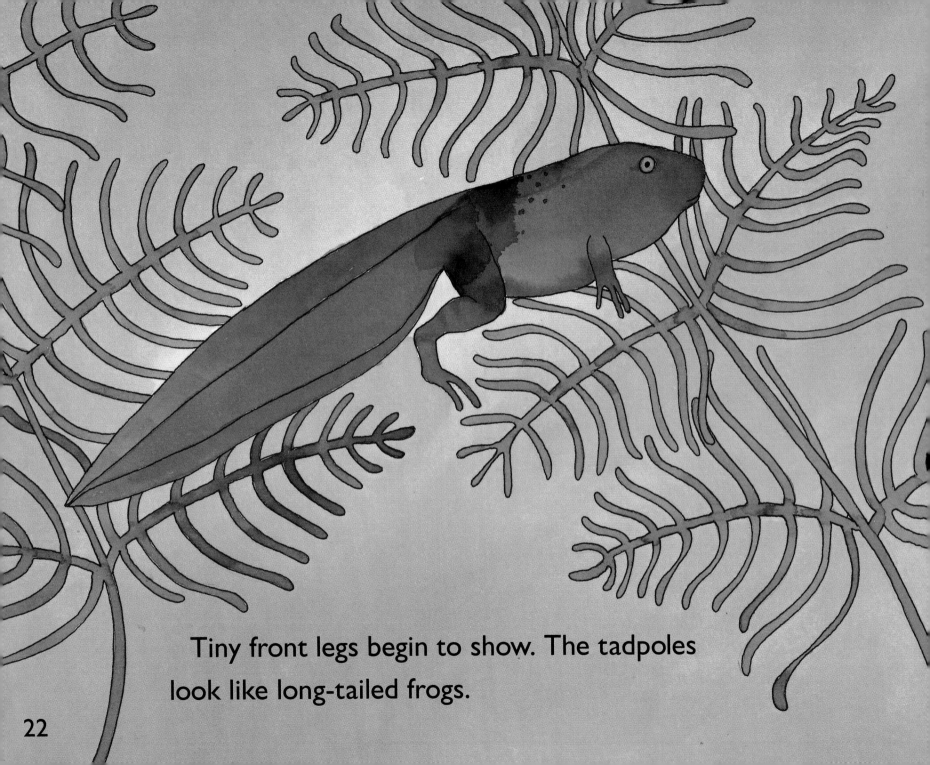

Tiny front legs begin to show. The tadpoles
look like long-tailed frogs.

All summer, the tadpoles change more—lungs
develop—and more—mouths and eyes grow
larger—and more—until they become frogs.

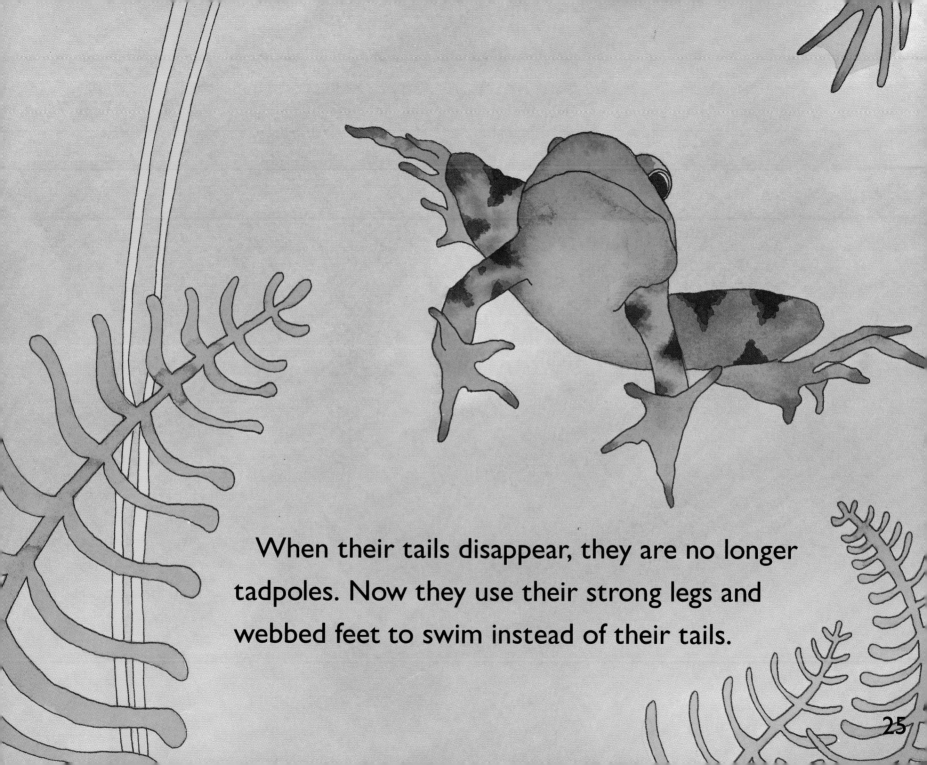

When their tails disappear, they are no longer tadpoles. Now they use their strong legs and webbed feet to swim instead of their tails.

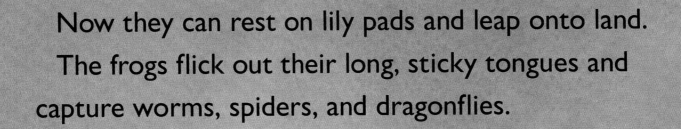

Now they can rest on lily pads and leap onto land. The frogs flick out their long, sticky tongues and capture worms, spiders, and dragonflies.

Now where are the frogs?

Slowly, the days grow colder. Winter winds blow.

Birds fly south. Once again the pond creatures

hibernate.

Where are the frogs now?

There are about 2000 kinds of frogs. They are different in size, shape, habits, and color. But they are alike in many ways. All frogs grow from eggs to legless fishlike tadpoles to four-legged adults.

The frog pictured throughout this book is a bullfrog. It is the largest frog in the United States. The bullfrog tadpole takes up to two years to change into a frog. Other tadpoles take anywhere from two weeks to two years to change into frogs.

Here are some other kinds of frogs.

Leopard or Grass Frog ▶

Leopard frogs are the most common frogs in the United States. They are covered with leopardlike spots and have a deep chuckle.

◀ **Pickerel Frog**

Pickerel frogs are greenish brown with squarish dark-brown spots. Poison comes out of their skin. Snakes will not eat them.

Wood Frog

Wood frogs live in the woods.
They lay eggs in quiet woodland pools.
They are brownish with black "robbers'
masks" on their faces.

 ### Spring Peeper

Tiny spring peepers have loud clear
voices. They start to sing after the first
warm rain. Peepers are one of the first
signs of spring.

Gray Tree Frog ▶

Gray tree frogs live in trees and shrubs. They
come down only to lay eggs in nearby ponds or
streams. Their color changes to match the trees.
They can stay still for a long time, so their enemies
do not see them.

Where are the bullfrogs?

This map shows where bullfrogs live throughout the United States.